Building My Vocabulary

EMOTIONS

LET'S READ AV² BY WEIGL™ ADDED VALUE • AUDIO VISUAL

By Dayna Martin

www.av2books.com

Go to **www.av2books.com,** and enter this book's unique code.

BOOK CODE

AVF67384

AV² by Weigl brings you media enhanced books that support active learning.

AV² provides enriched content that supplements and complements this book. Weigl's AV² books strive to create inspired learning and engage young minds in a total learning experience.

Your AV² Media Enhanced books come alive with...

Audio
Listen to sections of the book read aloud.

Video
Watch informative video clips.

Embedded Weblinks
Gain additional information for research.

Try This!
Complete activities and hands-on experiments.

Key Words
Study vocabulary, and complete a matching word activity.

Quizzes
Test your knowledge.

Slide Show
View images and captions, and prepare a presentation.

... and much, much more!

Published by AV² by Weigl
350 5th Avenue, 59th Floor New York, NY 10118
Website: www.av2books.com

Library of Congress Cataloging-in-Publication Data

Names: Martin, Dayna, 1983- author.
Title: Emotions / Dayna Martin.
Description: New York, NY : AV2 by Weigl, [2019] | Series: Building my vocabulary
Identifiers: LCCN 2018053449 (print) | LCCN 2018055557 (ebook) | ISBN 9781489696519 (Multi User Ebook) | ISBN 9781489696526 (Single User Ebook) | ISBN 9781489696496 (hardcover : alk. paper) | ISBN 9781489696502 (softcover : alk. paper)
Subjects: LCSH: Emotions in children--Juvenile literature. | Emotions--Juvenile literature.
Classification: LCC BF723.E6 (ebook) | LCC BF723.E6 M367 2019 (print) | DDC 155.4/124--dc23
LC record available at https://lccn.loc.gov/2018053449

Printed in the United States of America in Brainerd, Minnesota
1 2 3 4 5 6 7 8 9 0 22 21 20 19 18

122018
102918

First published by Engage Books in 2015

Project Coordinator: Priyanka Das Designer: A.R. Roumanis

The publisher acknowledges Shutterstock as the primary image supplier for this title.

EMOTIONS

by Dayna Martin

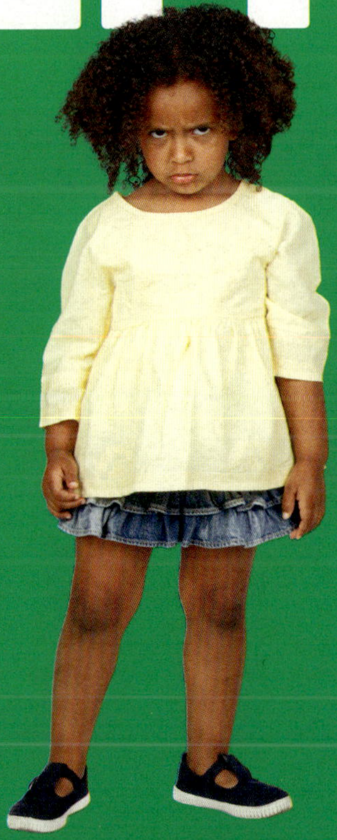

Anger

Brave

Love

Jealous

Scared

Pride

Frustration

Shock

Grumpy

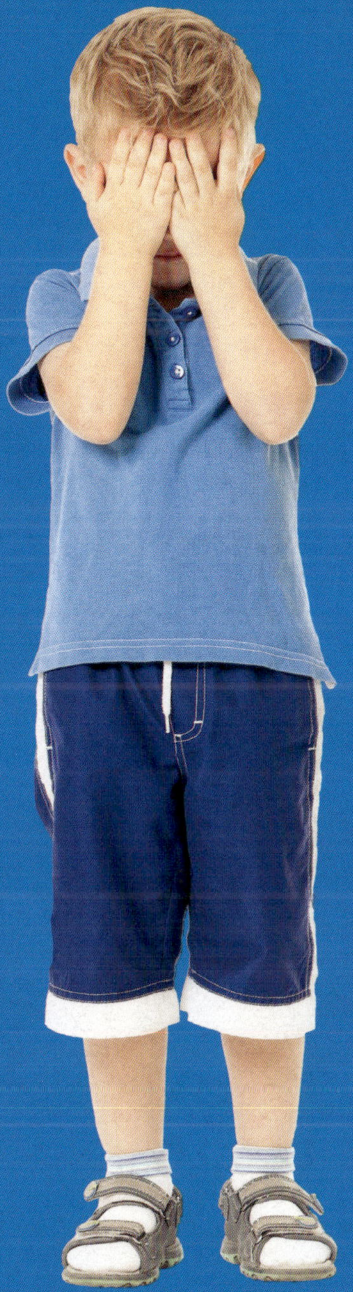

Shy

Annoyed

Hope

Sad

Sleepy

Silly

Judgment

Guilt

Nervous

Pouty

Wonder

Surprise

Depressed

Disgust

Hurt

Happy

Bored

Sorry

Emotions activity

Do you know what these emotions and expressions are called? Can you find **happy, love, surprise, sleepy, scared, anger, brave, sad,** and **shock**? Match the names to the pictures.

Answer: shock

Answer: scared

Answer: sleepy

Answer: surprise

Answer: brave

Answer: happy

Answer: anger

Answer: sad

Answer: love